How To Manage Money

Strategies For Debt Repayment, Establishing Financial Objectives, And Cultivating Wealth

(How To Establish A Target For Savings And Craft An Achievable Budget)

Sebastien Chisholm

TABLE OF CONTENT

Introduction..1

How To Maintain The Passiveness Of Your Income Sources 26

Which Category Of Passive Income Requires Greater Consideration..30

The Most Prominent Determinant Of An Online Passive Income Stream 35

The Advantages Of Pursuing A Supplementary Income Source 61

How To Increase Your Wealth While Safeguarding Every Euro 91

Keep An Account As You Shop........................... 133

Introduction

In contemporary society, the foundation of our social structure lies in the realm of finances. Due to financial resources, individuals are afforded the opportunity to lead a fulfilling life, pursue personal endeavors, and establish a family. Financial resources are crucial for the pursuit of our aspirations and the satisfaction of our fundamental necessities, including sustenance, shelter, and apparel, as well as our discretionary desires, such as exploring new destinations or acquiring technologically advanced devices.

In the absence of financial resources, one would be unable to satisfy any of these necessities.

However, the funds frequently prove to be insufficient. The cumulative monthly fixed expenditures, encompassing essentials such as sustenance, utility bills, and transportation costs, alongside the unforeseen incidents like vehicle malfunctions, computer repairs, or dental visits, consistently loom on the horizon. How can we effectively execute prudent financial management to accumulate savings that enable us to attain true fiscal autonomy rather than reaching the brink of insolvency towards the end of each month?

Various approaches to achieve fiscal savings exist, alongside efficient methods to generate substantial earnings expeditiously.

Engaging in illicit activities such as drug trafficking, arms dealing, or other unlawful ventures may lead to a potential outcome of incarceration. These endeavors prove to be lucrative if one can establish a thriving business enterprise. Alternatively, you have the option to employ workers who can serve as proxies for your drug trade, allowing you to remain at home and indulge in a life of opulence.

All of these circumstances may lead to your eventual arrest or demise at the hands of a rival.

Alternatively, you may consider pursuing a career as a stock market operator, attempting to mirror the success of Leonardo Di Caprio's character in the movie "The Wolf of Wall Street" and establish a prosperous empire worth millions. Engaging in stock market operations appears to be straightforward, as online tutorials articulate strategies for generating substantial returns swiftly, thereby rendering failure unattainable.

In doing so, you will exclusively encounter unfavorable investment opportunities, leading to the depletion of your financial assets.

You may also consider venturing into the online betting industry. You possess a profound interest in soccer or football, being well-versed in its historical context, and consistently staying informed of the outcome of every match. You have the potential to generate revenue from this passion by investing a significant amount of money on a seemingly implausible outcome. Eventually, you are bound to win a bet and accrue substantial wealth. It is feasible to explore a trustworthy methodology, ensuring consistent victories.

Ultimately, one will inevitably incur losses in all gambling endeavors. The incidence of triumphs will be exceedingly infrequent, and ultimately, you will incur substantial financial losses that surpass your earnings.

These three instances epitomize irony, yet the underlying message remains unequivocal: making money easily, if at all possible, is not viable through legitimate means. Earning money should invariably originate from employment. In this book, we shall also delve into strategies that complement your revenue through additional endeavors. However, it is imperative to emphasize that the crux of your economic stability lies in the effective administration of your present finances.

Effectively managing your financial affairs is the initial stride towards attaining financial independence. Effectively Preserve and Allocate Your

Finances to Experience the Illusion of Doubling Your Wealth.

What Is Financial Freedom?

In essence, it pertains to the economic accessibility one possesses in order to sustain their chosen lifestyle without harboring concerns about financial matters. In order to achieve genuine financial freedom, it is essential that your monthly savings surpass a minimum of 50% of your total expenses. By employing this approach, you will effectively manage any unforeseen expenses and fulfill your desires accordingly.

A highly effective approach towards attaining financial independence involves the diversification of income streams, encompassing various sources of revenue, while efficiently managing expenditures and maintaining a well-structured monthly budget.

The importance of diversifying investments lies in its ability to ensure varied returns, which can mitigate the impact of income loss or unforeseen circumstances.

What strategies can one adopt to attain this state of financial independence?

Moreover, acquiring the skill of effectively managing your monthly finances will necessitate the pursuit of investment diversification. A highly effective strategy for diversifying one's investments and generating additional streams of income lies in harnessing the power of the internet and leveraging the myriad of opportunities it presents.

Commence an e-commerce venture by engaging in the sale of products on reputable platforms such as eBay or Amazon, or alternatively, consider leveraging Amazon's affiliate program by incorporating it into your Facebook profile or blog. Select a specialized market segment that aligns with your personal interests (your genuine enthusiasm is highly valuable) and proceed to discuss this industry by highlighting the most sought-after products of the era through effective promotional efforts. The affiliate program comprises a hyperlink that will redirect users to the advertised product, and upon a successful transaction, the program will attribute a percentage of the sale to your account.

Alternatively, if you possess strong translation, graphic design, or SEO skills, you could commence a professional journey as a freelance professional on renowned platforms like Guru or Upwork.

If you have a passion for writing, you have the opportunity to publish an eBook on Kindle and generate income from each sale. Alternatively, you can establish a YouTube channel and monetize it through the inclusion of advertisements within your videos.

There are numerous legitimate opportunities that can be pursued on the internet to generate additional income. However, it takes considerable time for these activities to become a lucrative revenue stream, requiring a substantial audience base, a significant number of visitors, numerous likes, and extensive contacts to generate sufficient advertising income.

Chapter Five: Thirteen Practices to Enhance Your Financial Intelligence Quotient.

The deeper you delve into the realm of personal finance, enhancing your financial intelligence quotient, the higher your likelihood of drawing increased monetary abundance into your existence. Presented herein are thirteen tangible strategies to augment your income, enabling you to cultivate wealth and establish enduring financial stability.

Regardless of gender, individuals are required to be responsible for their own personal belongings, including their handbags, which in turn signifies the importance of effectively managing their finances. Personal finance has the potential to yield great rewards and grant a sense of freedom and independence, barring the circumstance where one lacks a fundamental understanding of the subject matter. If such is indeed your identity, be not perturbed, for these six strategies for enhancing your financial intelligence shall facilitate the acquisition of greater knowledge pertaining to monetary matters, thereby enabling the accumulation of wealth in your life.

If your aim is to have a successful year, there are numerous strategies to achieve that outcome. You can address high-interest debt, establish an emergency fund, and allocate funds for a specific purpose. There are a few items on your financial agenda that you can swiftly address, taking no longer than five minutes.

In general, the imperative to cultivate a transformative mindset becomes paramount when striving to generate prosperity. If one fails to acquire further knowledge about financial matters, how can they make enduring improvements or prevent the repetition of past errors? If You Seek to Enhance Your Financial Intelligence, Here Are Thirteen Habits to Adopt in the Coming Year.

Read About Personal Finance

Many individuals embarking on their journey to learn personal finance often commence by delving into a well-established and reputable book on the topic. Prominent choices for reading material in this subject area consist of renowned titles such as Robert Kiyosaki's "Rich Dad, Poor Dad," David Bach's "The Automatic Millionaire," and Dave Ramsey's "The Total Money Makeover." However, there exist numerous alternative literary selections that can facilitate a shift in one's mindset pertaining to financial matters. Acquire one (or two) pertaining to financial matters that align with your objectives, be it budgeting, debt repayment, or investing.

Track Your Net Worth

Establish Your Financial Objectives Prioritarily. I Have Heard That You Should Dependably Keep Running With The Objective In Mind. Great Exhortation. Subsequently, it is imperative that you exercise vigilant oversight over your personal progress, encompassing both your personal development, professional advancement, and overall financial standing. Without current awareness, it becomes challenging to ascertain whether you are making progress towards your objectives. I previously employed a spreadsheet as a means of organizing my data; however, the burden of continuously updating it proved too cumbersome, prompting me to discontinue its use. Subsequently, I came across Personal Capital, which has effectively automated the majority of these tasks. Not only does it provide real-time updates on my net worth, but it also sends me notifications regarding my expenses.

Track Your Spending

Are you ready to experience a profound transformation in your financial well-being? Monitor Your Expenditures Temporarily. This exercise requires a modest amount of physical exertion, yet it effectively illustrates the destination of your financial resources. Regardless of whether you maintain a meticulous record of your expenditures, utilize banking services, make credit card statements, or employ specialized software, you will be unable to conceal the true extent of your monthly spending on sustenance, entertainment, and miscellaneous items once you gain awareness of the actual figures.

Schedule a Consultation with a Financial Advisor and/or Tax Consultant

As your financial situation becomes increasingly complex, it is advisable to consult with a financial specialist who specializes in optimizing investments. They can provide valuable insights and strategies that may be unfamiliar to you. Alternatively, meeting with an accountant or tax advisor has its own advantages, particularly given the upcoming changes in tax regulations. In an ideal scenario, you would be required to make the minimal payment charge... Without Breaking The Law. A professional task coordinator can facilitate such actions for you, while also assisting in reducing future liabilities.

Move Your Thinking

Frequently, our thought processes confine us within a realm where our intellectual development remains stagnant. To enhance your knowledge and competence in financial matters, it is imperative to shift your mindset. Direct your focus towards the long-term value of structured wealth, rather than fixating on presently expensive possessions that you perceive as indispensable. When one's focus is directed towards spending, it hampers the development of their financial intelligence. However, once an individual shifts their mindset towards finding avenues to augment their wealth, they will experience a growth in their financial acumen and begin making decisions that align with such a mentality. Enhancing one's quick-wittedness entails cultivating sharper cognitive acuity!

Invest Your Time Wisely

Enhancing your financial intelligence necessitates dedicating sufficient time to diligently undertake the necessary tasks to enhance your financial circumstances. In order to achieve financial wellness, it is imperative to exhibit proficiency in managing one's finances. Liberating oneself from debt will enhance one's financial intelligence, just as effectively managing one's habitual expenditures will have the same effect. Rather than idly waiting and speculating about the affordability of your needs, adopt a proactive approach by allocating a portion of your monthly income towards structuring your finances. Achieve this by faithfully documenting your incoming funds and meticulously planning how they will be utilized. Engaging in this activity provides a more extensive experience compared to transferring your funds.

Invest In Yourself

Perhaps it would be beneficial for you to consider enrolling in a different course in order to acquire new perspectives. Alternatively, obtaining a certification could potentially enhance your earning potential and open up promising career opportunities. On rare occasions, the most valuable financial resource an individual can possess is not in the form of bonds or stocks, but rather lies in the pursuit of personal development. Indeed, what superior asset could be employed for wealth creation than yourself?

Network

By actively participating in industry-specific events and engaging with professionals in your field, you stay well-informed about the latest developments in your industry and establish valuable connections. One can never predict when a new romantic connection may lead to a flourishing opportunity for employment, affiliation with a reputable organization, or a promising career prospect.

Direct your attention to what is within your jurisdiction.

At times, life may seem tumultuous and capricious. Irrespective of the extent to which you acquire knowledge concerning financial matters, it remains beyond your control to influence stock market movements or the potential depreciation of your property. Given the substantial extent beyond our control, many individuals question the feasibility of striving for financial well-being. Nevertheless, do not succumb to despair: directing your focus towards elements within your control will ultimately prove advantageous. As an illustration, although one does not have the ability to alter the rhythmic fluctuations of the stock market, one has the capacity to exercise control over the quantity of one's investments. Additionally, in the event that you do not have control over whether you receive a salary increase in your professional setting, you do possess the ability to govern the manner in which you allocate your earnings.

Allocate funds towards participation in financial seminars, workshops, and conferences

Certain financial institutions offer complimentary workshops that can serve as an effective means to enhance your financial literacy. Similarly, affordable financial education courses can be found at local community colleges, corporations, and various organizations. There is no need for you to contemplate investment strategies or immerse yourself in accounting textbooks in order to attract more wealth into your life. Simply start acquiring knowledge about successful financial outcomes and focus on the abundance of money that is available (as there is a substantial amount to be obtained).

Engage in discussions with stockbrokers, real estate agents, investment advisors, and personal finance advisors.

Inquire extensively about any and all topics that come to mind. People derive satisfaction from sharing their expertise, and individuals in the field of finance are aware of the general public's limited financial knowledge. The greater the number of inquiries you raise, the more information you will acquire pertaining to personal finance... and consequently, the more at ease you will become with the outcomes of your financial decisions.

Please enroll in either one of the financial periodicals or newspapers.

Please visit your local library and borrow a variety of financial publications. If you come across a topic that captures your interest, make a commitment to explore it further or make it a habit to regularly access the library's most recent publications. Develop a habit of reading and studying about money and finances. Furthermore, gain insight into the ways in which prudent debt management can contribute to achieving financial prosperity.

Engage in extensive reading or audio consumption of a diverse range of literature pertaining to financial matters. In addition to personal involvement, the most effective approach to acquire knowledge is to access expert information. Numerous resources such as audiotapes, printed books, CDs, ebooks, and Kindle books are available on passive income sources, enhancing financial abundance, land investment, debt reduction, early retirement, understanding money personality, resolving financial conflicts in marriages, stock market participation, common fund investment, and numerous other topics. To enhance your financial intelligence, it is not necessary to read every finance book from beginning to end, but maintaining a consistent reading habit can be beneficial. You shall retain the information absorbed through your reading endeavors and progress steadfastly toward achieving your financial goals.

One has the ability to become their own hero.

Relying on others to rescue you is a fallacy as no one possesses a better understanding of the required actions than you do. Occasionally, assistance can prove to be quite useful. Your Best Savior Is You Because You Can Also Be Your Own Hero.

There is no necessity for you to don an extraordinary uniform or engage in combat with adversaries possessing exceptional abilities. It is adequate to devote one's attention and prioritize self-care during moments of utmost necessity. Alternatively, if not addressed, a sense of unease or discomfort could potentially manifest in the future and become a permanent fixture.

Taking charge of your own destiny and assuming the role of protagonist in your life journey will undoubtedly facilitate the enhancement of your self-worth, propel you towards the realization of your aspirations, and unequivocally demonstrate to others that you possess the capacity to accomplish whatever you aspire. Your Happiness Depends On Yourself And Definitely On Your Heroism.

The Significance of Decision-Making

A hero can be characterized by their courage, their capacity to take action, and, to some extent, their capability to foster joy and welfare. What are the methods employed by a protagonist to accomplish this task? Through exercising decision-making abilities, one can delineate their actions and destinations, signifying that the significance of one's choices cannot be understated when aspiring to become one's own champion.

The issue at hand is that you tend to inadvertently make decisions on a regular basis, often without realizing it. This encompasses a wide range of choices ranging from selecting your attire and deciding on your meals to planning out your daily activities. Your daily regimen is replete with a multitude of choices. The optimal choices are contingent upon our demeanor. What considerations inform your approach towards each day, or more precisely, how do you navigate and manage the unfolding of events?

Frequently, an individual may erroneously perceive themselves as possessing less authority than they actually hold over the course of their own lives. Hence, establishing your course of action and discerning your stance towards various circumstances is of paramount importance. A vigilant individual acknowledges the presence of this inherent strength and endeavors to nurture it. Shall we embark on our tasks?

Cease granting authority to those inner voices that impede progress and confine you within the confines of your comfort zone. Alternatively, opt to safeguard yourself from this malevolent commodity.

The Protagonist and the Antagonists

In addition to their courageous spirit, a hero is characterized by their unwavering commitment to combat adversaries and ultimately preserve the world. To achieve self-empowerment, it is imperative to acquire the skills necessary to combat adversities that emerge within oneself.

Who Are Your Enemies? All entities and individuals that cause you distress and discomfort, as well as anything or anyone that undermines your dignity and worth. This encompasses apprehensions, lack of faith, disagreements, and detrimental dynamics. But, Above All, Yourself. Each instance in which you subject yourself to mistreatment or neglect self-reflection, you inadvertently overlook the immense potential residing within you.

Do I have to engage in an internal struggle? No, contrary to the heroes portrayed in media, it is essential to transmute any adversities into endeavors that foster personal welfare. Alternatively, or perhaps more aptly, into something from which valuable lessons can always be gleaned. Your ordeal is not a battle, but rather a quest for understanding and mindfulness, enabling you to change the trajectory of your circumstances and begin prioritizing self-care. That's The Key.

What steps can I take to embody the role of a protagonist in my own life?

We have previously observed that cultivating mindfulness of one's choices and fostering a holistic mindset towards acquiring consciousness, which can then be harnessed as a supportive accomplice, represents a significant endeavor towards personal heroism. Furthermore, what other course of action do you have at your disposal?

It is crucial to initiate the analysis of the factors and individuals exerting control over your life. Are the primary influences in your life attributable to your employer, your family, your occupation, or societal norms? When did you grant unequivocal consent for unrestricted control over your person?

We don't intend to imply that all individuals in your vicinity are now adversaries. Rather, what we intend to convey is that occasionally these individuals can pose hindrances in your journey towards personal development, even though their intentions are genuinely good. Therefore, it is crucial to stay vigilant of your surroundings so as to avoid being unduly influenced by them in a detrimental manner.
The pathway to becoming the protagonist of your own narrative lies within, rather than outside of yourself. It

exists internally, residing within the depths of every individual. It encompasses the potential to acknowledge oneself and bestow upon oneself the necessary recognition to procure enhanced self-care. Since there exists solely one individual who will remain by your side indefinitely, through both favorable and unfavorable circumstances. And the individual in question happens to be none other than yourself. Engaging in self-criticism and self-sabotage proves to be an inefficient and unproductive use of time.

Ensure your own well-being, cultivate self-love, and strive to comprehend your own being. Genuine heroes are not the ones engaged in perpetual battles against creatures or soaring amidst the clouds. Heroes are individuals who possess the capacity to rescue themselves on a daily basis, driven by the objective of attaining a rewarding existence and bestowing joy upon those in their immediate circles.

How To Maintain The Passiveness Of Your Income Sources

Passive income is regarded as the most advantageous form of income worldwide. Numerous channels for passive income and opportunities can enable individuals to attain their desired possessions and aspirations. They Can Allow You To Live The Life That You Want. Nevertheless, numerous individuals experience a transition from passive income sources to active income sources, necessitating diligent management and substantial effort.

The objective of this article is to provide you with advice on maintaining the passivity of your income sources. This section pertains to real estate investments, which were previously my preferred passive income avenue and have now become my new source of income.

Listed below are several recommendations for effectively

maintaining the passive nature of your income sources:

Pursue singles instead of home runs.

I possess real estate investments that I had anticipated would yield exceptionally high returns. Effectively administering affordable housing for individuals with low incomes can yield these outcomes; however, in the absence of caution, one may encounter the unintended consequence of experiencing a significant monthly financial drain despite one's diligent efforts.

Despite having employed a property manager to handle all aspects, I ultimately incurred financial losses and experienced numerous difficulties.

Be prepared to dedicate a significant amount of effort initially.

Many People Believe That Passive Income Sources Are Passive From Day 1. Nevertheless, such an approach proves ineffective. In order to gain entry to and attain a comprehensive comprehension of genuinely passive revenue streams, it is imperative to diligently engage in self-education or invest significant effort right from the outset. This may appear as a substantial amount of effort when compared to the initial outcomes, however, the long-term rewards will be significant.

Eliminate Or Minimize Variables:

This Constitutes the Authentic Key to Maintaining the Passivity of Income Sources. I am burdened with the responsibilities associated with my properties, such as managing tenants, ensuring code compliance, overseeing electricity matters, attending to repairs, and maintaining accurate accounting records. Due to the multitude of variables that must be mastered, achieving true passivity in these real estate investments proves to be a challenging endeavor. Identify opportunities in which a significant number of variables have been effectively managed.

While real estate has been a preferred source of passive income for an extended period of time, I have made the decision to divert a significant portion of my attention towards network marketing as it provides me with the opportunity to establish a business at my own desired pace. It necessitates a substantial investment of effort initially to yield significant returns in the future, and it is the sole industry I am aware of where the majority of variables are managed.

Which Category Of Passive Income Requires Greater Consideration

Establishing a sustainable source of passive income presents a significant undertaking that necessitates diligent focus and careful cultivation.

There are various categories of passive income; some fall under the category of active passive income, which require extensive preparation and hard work before actual financial gains are realized, while others belong to the realm of true passive income methods that operate on established systems and do not entail the arduous labor associated with active passive income approaches.

Nevertheless, the maintenance and management of these residual income streams will necessitate your continual attention and effort. It is uncertain whether you will be able to anticipate the extent of work that may be required. One must exercise great caution as a result.

In this context, you will delve into the various categories of income-generating methodologies that demand heightened concentration and the underlying rationales thereof for an individual operating as an entrepreneur. Continuing to read will allow you to delve into the rationale, the necessary steps, and additional information regarding the development of a well-crafted plan.

Why Various Forms of Residual Income Deserve Greater Consideration: Elucidated in Layman's Terms

Since you have already delved into the two primary forms of passive income, it is expected that you have also comprehended the adjustments required to sustain these revenue streams. A

Simultaneously, the aforementioned titles encapsulate the essence; active and passive income methods require divergent degrees of focus, necessitating frequent modifications and heightened exertions from an entrepreneur, whereas passive income methods that demand diminished attention are regarded as genuine passive income sources. An examination of the reasons behind the need for increased attention towards these active residual income methods.

1. They face increased competition. 2. They are confronted with a larger number of competitors. 3. They have a greater number of rivals vying against them. 4. They encounter heightened competition from numerous competitors. 5. Their market is saturated with more competitors.

Undoubtedly, the income opportunities that yield higher profits are subjected to a substantial amount of competition. The Active Residual Income Methods have the potential to generate substantial profits within a short period of time, thereby making it an immensely competitive industry. If you are operating such enterprise, it is imperative that you maintain a competitive edge in order to maximize profitability.

It is essential for you to comprehend the evolving consumer trends and behaviors in order to optimize your profitability. Consequently, conducting thorough research is imperative. Therefore, it is imperative to enhance your level of focus, adopt a more attentive mindset, allocate greater amounts of time and financial resources in order to effectively manage and flourish your business.

The earnings potential is uncapped, offering limitless opportunities.

Given your absence of earning caps, it is evident that you consistently have the opportunity to optimize your profitability. Failure to maintain proactive engagement and keep pace with the surrounding environment will inevitably result in financial losses.

Therefore, it is imperative to maintain a heightened level of focus and exercise utmost caution when considering the decisions and actions you are undertaking for the advancement of your business. Once again, the strategy at hand is straightforward: increased financial resources necessitate heightened dedication, and greater dedication demands heightened focus.

3. There are advancements in the evolution and further development of existing methods.

Ultimately, these active income opportunities are constantly undergoing transformation. You must ensure that the businesses are undergoing continuous advancements and that you are actively implementing measures to enhance the success and value of your business.

If you seek to advance the growth of your business, it is imperative that you allocate increased attention, financial resources, and time towards that endeavor. That concept is straightforward, which is precisely why active passive income businesses require increased attention and exertion.

The Most Prominent Determinant Of An Online Passive Income Stream

A business owner must attend to a multitude of obligations in order to ensure seamless functionality. There are multiple factors that exert significant influence on each online passive income business. The business proprietor must remain informed about the alterations, fluctuations, and requisite adjustments in order to maintain a competitive edge.

Nonetheless, it is imperative for him to prioritize several fundamental factors to enhance the potency and gratification of his online passive income stream. The most prominent aspect of a passive income business is its ability to operate autonomously.

If you are able to establish proper configuration and synchronize all components as necessary, you will achieve self-sufficiency in the system, resulting in long-term sustainability for your passive income venture. Within these pages, you will delve deeper into the concept of the sustainability of a passive income business and uncover the most influential factor pertaining to its online presence.

Operating autonomously is the most influential factor in establishing a passive revenue channel on the internet.

The most advantageous aspect of a passive income business lies in its fully automated system, capable of functioning without any supervision or with minimal oversight. This aspect is also regarded as one of the most influential factors that render it passive and highly lucrative for an online business entrepreneur.

Given that the business operation operates autonomously, the proprietor can devote their attention towards the expansion of their enterprise and the augmentation of their financial gains. The following elucidates how the automatization of a business operation facilitates the business's online growth.

1. It enables the organization to establish a distinct objective and concentrate its efforts. 2. It aids the business in defining a precise goal and maintaining concentration. 3. It facilitates the establishment of a clear target and concentration for the organization. 4. It assists the business in setting a well-defined objective and maintaining focus. 5. It supports the organization in having a precise target and concentrated effort. 6. It allows the business to have a clear focus and well-defined goals. 7. It helps the organization establish a specific target and maintain focus. 8. It assists the business in attaining a clear objective and concentration.

Since the business operation is fully automated, it possesses a distinct objective and can readily prioritize raw data over factors such as assumptions and market conditions.

This is precisely why a business is capable of independently overcoming any challenges as and when required, and the business owner can confidently rely on the system without any semblance of uncertainty. This fosters productivity, ultimately leading to increased financial gains. If one is inclined to dedicate attention to the advancement of their business, it is imperative to establish a system that facilitates autonomous and independent operation.

The entrepreneur can swiftly assess the strengths and weaknesses with great ease.

While managing a passive income business, the business entrepreneur possesses comprehensive knowledge about the operations, obtaining additional time to acquire a profound understanding of the synchronicity of various aspects. He possesses a deep understanding of both the most formidable aspect and the most vulnerable aspect of his business endeavor.

Hence, he is able to swiftly investigate any matters when necessary. If it becomes necessary for you to oversee every individual operation, you would be deprived of the invaluable opportunity to observe your business operations in such a favorable manner. Business entrepreneurs who are managing a passive business have the ability to resolve issues at a faster pace than initially anticipated.

The business owner or manager can direct their efforts towards expanding or developing the venture.

Ultimately, this is the most captivating aspect that every passive online business has to provide. The business owner or manager can conveniently direct their attention towards business development, marketing, and branding, thereby evidently increasing profitability.

That's why a significant number of prominent business corporations are currently endeavoring to implement automation in their operations, with the aim of dedicating the majority of their time and creative energy to these critical matters and advancing their business to a higher echelon.

An Active Approach

Personal financial management will continue to be a perpetual and never-ending endeavor unless one possesses the means to engage the assistance of professional finance managers. Money management should not be regarded as a one-time event, nor should it be treated as a mere occasion. Engaging consistently in this ongoing endeavor is necessary for individuals to enhance their financial well-being. Two strategies for effectively managing finances encompass goal achievement and proactive decision-making, both of which will significantly enhance your financial situation.

Achieving Goals

To actualize your financial aspirations, it is imperative to establish them as a primary step. Identifying your objectives may present challenges at times. In order to arrive at a well-informed decision regarding the prioritization of your financial goals, it is crucial to ascertain the specific actions that will yield the most significant returns. For instance, as mentioned previously, opting to make a payment towards a credit card with a 20% interest rate would be a more prudent choice compared to making a payment on a credit card with a 10% interest rate but the same outstanding balance. Effectively organizing your financial documents will significantly aid you in establishing suitable objectives, which serves as the initial stride towards accomplishing them.

When establishing your financial objectives, it is imperative to ascertain your personal priorities. Finite resources necessitate the need for you to make decisions regarding their allocation. As an illustration, numerous individuals with good intentions emphasize the welfare of their pets and children above fulfilling their financial obligations, such as credit card payments. To exemplify, individuals of this nature may allocate additional funds towards the purchase of high-quality dog food while potentially compromising their capacity to promptly settle their credit card obligations. While it is advisable to strive towards attaining a state of debt-free existence and a favorable net worth, the establishment of your priorities will play a crucial role in formulating your financial objectives.

For the purpose of this exercise, compile a list outlining the prominent factors that incur substantial financial costs in your life. As an illustration, one may consider incorporating in this compilation the essentials of survival, the well-being of children and pets, rental expenses, as well as transportation needs. Subsequently, proceed to prioritize them based on their level of significance. It is expected that you will make relentless efforts to accomplish each objective mentioned in the list. The assigned priority to each goal will serve as your guide for determining the sequential order in which you should pursue them. In view of this, it would be prudent to allocate some additional months for settling the hospital expenses, if it guarantees a consistent supply of nourishment for both yourself and your canine companion.

To accomplish your objectives, it is imperative to possess discipline. The act of establishing financial goals will provide you with a sense of purpose. Now, It Is Up To You To Dedicate Yourself To The Realization Of Those Goals. Do Not Cheat Yourself. During my college years, I did not possess substantial financial resources, yet I successfully avoided incurring any debt throughout that period. Simultaneously, I observed how one of my industrious colleagues persistently voiced dissatisfaction with her financial circumstances, yet exhibited a reluctance to exercise prudent judgement when it came to her expenditures. She would consistently allocate over fifty dollars per week to the exclusive purchase of cigarettes and premium alcoholic beverages. Subsequently, she frequently ventured to the mall in the company of her friends, indulging in the purchase of superfluous garments. It is evident that she prioritized her indulgences over her financial stability. To effectively pursue financial objectives, it is advisable to avoid repeating the mistakes commonly made by my acquaintance and numerous other students who have encountered unfortunate circumstances during their college years.

To attain your financial objectives, it is imperative that you adhere to a budget, exhibit self-honesty, and proactively pursue innovative methods to economize your finances.

Taking Action

One cannot achieve their financial objectives by remaining in the confines of their home, succumbing to despair over their circumstances. On the contrary, one must adopt a proactive approach when it comes to managing finances. The decisive factor between affluence and aspiring prosperity lies in one's proactive endeavors.

Therefore, commence your duties promptly.

First and foremost, grasp hold of the telephone and proceed to initiate the necessary communication by dialing the requisite numbers. If an excessive credit card balance burdens you, we recommend contacting your bank to inquire about the possibility of transferring the balance to a card offering a more favorable interest rate. If you believe that a debt consolidation loan would be advantageous for your financial situation, it is advisable to contact your preferred creditor and express your interest in obtaining a loan of this nature." "If you deem a debt consolidation loan as advantageous to your financial circumstances, it is recommended to initiate communication with your preferred creditor to inquire about the availability of such a loan." "If you perceive a debt consolidation loan as beneficial to improving your financial state, it is prudent to reach out to your preferred creditor and formally inquire about the possibility of securing a loan of this nature. You will not achieve any progress or advancement by remaining in bed and indulging in self-pity. There will be no one coming to your aid. The ability to transform your financial circumstances lies within your control.

Furthermore, Ensure Efficient Financial Management. It is highly likely that you will have fluctuating expenditures that require modification on a monthly basis. When encountering variables related to the budget, incorporate them into your financial plan. Subsequently, modify your expenditure patterns accordingly. It is not feasible to devise a single budget and anticipate its endurance over several months. It is probable that your expenditures and earnings will fluctuate on a monthly basis. It is your responsibility to accurately incorporate these changes into your budget as they arise.

Once you have arranged for automated payments for all of your outstanding and anticipated debts, enrolled in a direct deposit savings program, and implemented as many automated systems as reasonably feasible in your financial transactions, then you may consider adopting a passive approach to money management.

In earlier times, individuals did not always possess the privilege of sustaining themselves through a passive approach to their resources. Examine the Evolutionary Consequences of Financial Management. Many millennia in the past, our ancestral tribes did not have the privilege of utilizing financial tools such as credit cards and loans to sustain themselves in the absence of any accumulated wealth or assets. If a member of a tribal community were to exhaust their essential resources such as food or precious metals used for bartering, their innate survival instinct would drive them to procure the necessary resources for their continued survival. Illustratively, in the instance where a member of an indigenous community experiences a state of hunger, lacking any means to procure sustenance, their innate hunger would serve as a driving force, impelling them to actively pursue nourishment. In the event that individual fails to obtain sustenance, either through discovery or exchange, their survival would be jeopardized. To put it differently, the ancestral variant of debt eliminated from the hereditary pool individuals who possessed inadequate skills in financial management.

Nevertheless, in the contemporary era, individuals in our civilized society have been given the opportunity to acquire essential commodities such as sustenance, even if they lack the necessary financial resources to cover the cost. At present, consumers are able to make purchases using credit cards, thus relieving themselves of the immediate burden of payment until the subsequent month. To some extent, modern financial institutions have fostered a tendency among individuals to adopt a more passive stance towards debt repayment. Exercise caution against being deceived by the apparent ease and convenience offered by modern-day lenders. Maintain Financial Control by Initiating Appropriate Measures.

Furthermore, it is unlikely that you will achieve success if you persistently attribute your shortcomings to others. It is possible that you have inherited financial obligations as a result of the passing of a family member; it is conceivable that you may have experienced asset loss due to a legal dispute; it is also conceivable that you have incurred significant medical expenses following an unfortunate injury. The World May Present You with an Unfavorable Circumstance. Nonetheless, it is incumbent upon you to assume responsibility for your financial situation, despite any mitigating circumstances that may have led to its occurrence. It is in your best interest to acknowledge this fact as early as possible. Engaging in a state of despondency, harboring resentment towards the world for the unfavorable financial predicament it has imposed upon you, will not serve to benefit you in any way. Assuming accountability serves as the initial stride towards initiating decisive measures.

Naturally, should one reside in a nation wherein the national leaders hitherto amass the entirety of the wealth for their own benefit, any subsequent financial instability encountered could potentially be justifiably attributed. Nevertheless, Western nations present abundant financial opportunities for individuals who are willing to exert effort and dedication.

Save For You Retirement

Regardless of whether you have invested considerable time in your profession or are nearing its culmination, there are still opportunities for augmenting your financial savings.

The veracity concerning retirement planning is that, owing to the forces of compound interest, initiating savings at an earlier stage may result in superior financial prospects. It is imperative to acknowledge that you are not solitary in this endeavor, and there exist actionable measures to augment your retirement savings, irrespective of whether you initiated them late or have yet to commence." Additionally, you can rephrase the second sentence as: "Furthermore, it is paramount to recognize that there are proactive measures you can adopt to amplify your retirement savings, regardless of a delayed commencement or absence thereof. There is always an opportune moment to initiate any undertaking.

Please consider the subsequent suggestions in order to enhance your savings and work towards achieving the desired retirement, irrespective of your present life phase.

Put Today's Beginning First.

Commence saving to the maximum extent possible immediately, particularly if you are in the initial stages of allocating funds for retirement, and afford compound interest—an opportunity for your assets to generate earnings that are subsequently reinvested to generate further earnings—a favorable opportunity to operate in your favor. According to Greenberg, initiating the task at an earlier juncture will result in a more favorable outcome.

A modest initial investment has the potential to yield favorable outcomes.

Although they are allocating smaller amounts on each occasion, a 25-year-old individual who initiates savings at the age of 25 and sets aside $75 each month will possess a larger portfolio at the age of 65 compared to a 35-year-old who commences savings with a monthly contribution of $100. A smaller capital allocation made over an extended time period can yield more significant repercussions on investment results compared to a larger sum invested within a limited timeframe.

Contribute funds to augment your 401(K) retirement plan.

If you meet the necessary qualifications and your place of employment provides a conventional 401(k) scheme, you potentially have the opportunity to make pre-tax contributions, affording you a significant advantage. Suppose one intends to allocate $100 per pay period and falls within the 12% tax bracket. Given that the mentioned funds are subtracted from your paycheck before the application of federal income taxes, your take-home pay will be diminished by a mere $88 (excluding any relevant state, local, social security, and Medicare taxes). This implies that you have the opportunity to enhance your investment without exerting a considerable influence on your monthly financial plan. Take into consideration your post-retirement income tax bracket to determine if opting for the Roth 401(K) feature, which invests revenue after taxes rather than pre-tax funds, would be the most suitable choice, provided that your employer's 401(K) plan incorporates such a feature. Even if you terminate your employment, there are still available courses of action to consider regarding the management of your 401(K) account.

Establish a Synergistic Connection with Your Employer.

If your employer presents the opportunity to match your 401(K) plan contributions, Greenberg advises that it is prudent to ensure that you contribute at least the minimum amount necessary to fully capitalize on the matching benefit. For instance, an employer may offer a commitment to contribute 50% of an employee's contributions, up to a maximum of 5% of their salary. Put simply, should you have an annual income of $50,000, and you allocate $2,500 from that to your retirement account, your employer will provide an extra $1,250 in contribution. Ultimately, it can be regarded as gratuitous funds. Please do not simply leave it in that place.

Start An IRA.

To assist in augmenting your savings, consider the possibility of initiating an Individual Retirement Account (IRA). Your two options consist of either a Standard IRA or a Roth IRA. Given the variability of your income and the eligibility of either you or your spouse for a corporate retirement scheme, a conventional IRA might be deemed as the most suitable alternative for your circumstances. It is feasible to obtain tax deductions for contributions made to a conventional IRA, and any gains generated from investments in the IRA possess the capability to grow without being subject to taxation until the time of retirement withdrawal. If your federal tax filing status places you within the phased-out modified adjusted gross income restrictions, a Roth IRA can serve as an intelligent choice for your financial planning. Please be advised that due to the post-tax nature of contributions to a Roth IRA, withdrawals made after reaching the age of 59 1/2 years are exempt from federal taxes and, subject to satisfying specific holding period criteria, may also be exempt from state taxes. Explore options to determine the most suitable IRA for your needs and review the latest 401(k) and IRA contribution limits to ascertain which type of IRA would be the best match for your requirements.

If you are of age 50 or above, it is advisable to make use of catch-up contributions.

Given that the limitations imposed on annual contributions to Individual Retirement Accounts (IRAs) and 401(k) plans are fixed, it is imperative to commence saving at the earliest opportunity. The favorable news is that individuals become eligible for catch-up contributions to IRAs and 401(k)s upon reaching the age of 50, starting from the corresponding calendar year. Consequently, if one has not been able to amass the desired amount of retirement savings throughout the years, the utilization of catch-up contributions can prove to be beneficial.

Make Savings Automatic.

It is highly probable that you are familiar with the proverb "Pay Yourself First." Greenberg suggests that by setting up automated monthly retirement contributions, you can potentially enhance your savings effortlessly. With the incorporation of the Merrill Automatic Investment Plan, which executes investment of cash automatically, you have the opportunity to streamline and automate your investment allocation preferences.

Limit Your Spending.

Check Your Spending Plan. One can potentially reduce expenses by negotiating for a reduced vehicle insurance premium or preparing and bringing lunch to work instead of buying it. Utilizing Merrill's Cash Flow Calculator can aid in identifying areas where spending can be trimmed, allowing for greater savings or investment opportunities.

Set A Target.

Having a clear understanding of your potential financial requirements can enhance the gratification of saving while simultaneously deepening your comprehension of the underlying reasons behind your savings endeavors. Establish Milestones Throughout the

Journey and Experience a Sense of Achievement as You Progress Towards Your Retirement. To assist you in determining the optimal time for retirement and the necessary investment and savings plan to achieve it, we recommend utilizing the Personal Retirement Calculator.

Save Any Extra Money.

Extra Cash? Exercise prudence in managing your resources. Enhance the Proportion of Your Donation with Every Increment in Income. A minimum allocation of 50 percent of the supplementary funds is required for deposit into your retirement plan account. While it may be enticing to allocate the tax refund or bonus funds towards a leisurely vacation or the purchase of a luxurious designer handbag, Greenberg strongly discourages such actions. Rather, she advises against considering these additional funds as unexpected windfall. Her suggestion is to indulge oneself with a modest purchase and employ the remaining funds to make substantial strides towards attaining your retirement objective.

The Advantages Of Pursuing A Supplementary Income Source

If you are interested in augmenting your income beyond your primary occupation, as per our desired objective, or if you wish to venture into a new endeavor, the concept of a side hustle may be considered. In order to embark on a fruitful side hustle, it is imperative that you first ascertain your interests and devise a sustainable approach. Possessing a wide array of ideas and comprehensive knowledge about side hustles can offer you the potential to amass greater financial resources while concurrently engaging in a pursuit that resonates with your personal inclinations, thereby affording you enhanced autonomy over your daily schedule. In the subsequent chapter, we will explore the concept of a side hustle, elucidate its advantageous aspects, and furnish illustrations of side hustles.

What constitutes a side hustle?
A side hustle refers to an additional form of employment pursued alongside an individual's primary full-time job, resulting in supplemental income. Engaging in a secondary entrepreneurial pursuit grants individuals greater autonomy and authority in determining their actions, schedule, and methodology. On occasion, one may even incorporate their personal interests into their supplementary enterprise, and ultimately witness its transformation into their principal vocation throughout the course of time.

ADVANTAGES OF ENGAGING IN A SUPPLEMENTARY OCCUPATION

Improves Your Finances
Thanks to the availability of side hustles, individuals have the opportunity to generate supplementary income alongside their primary employment. Supplementing your income provides

the opportunity to augment your savings and/or contribute towards other financial obligations. The Additional Profits Have the Potential to Expanding Your Supplementary Endeavor into a Significant Enterprise.

It has the potential to pave the way for a new professional trajectory for you.
Incorporating your passions into your side hustles is a prudent course of action. By delving into your passions, actively pursuing them, and integrating them into your supplementary endeavors, you afford yourself the opportunity to nurture them into a viable vocation. Cultivating specific skills is of utmost importance as they can significantly contribute to the success of your side business.

Gaining Flexibility
One benefit of engaging in a side hustle is the ability to acquire the flexibility of overseeing and organizing your own timetable. Given your capacity, you will be responsible for ensuring that your

side venture effectively accommodates your primary employment and any other pertinent obligations you may have. This advantage has the potential to aid you in attaining an excellent level of flexibility.

Provides the Benefit of Expanding Your Social Network
Engaging in a supplementary professional endeavor presents the opportunity to engage with individuals and establish valuable connections, which, in turn, may alleviate feelings of loneliness and isolation. Although this might not constitute the primary motive for individuals engaging in a side hustle. Engaging in uncomplicated supplementary ventures can serve as a genuine opportunity to initiate increased social interactions.

Facilitates the Acquisition of Novel Skills
When engaging in a supplementary source of income, it becomes essential to acquire a repertoire of additional competencies. It presents an opportunity to embark on a distinctive

venture that will greatly enhance your skillset beyond what you anticipate. One advantageous aspect of engaging in multiple side hustles is the ability to exercise autonomy and leverage this opportunity to further develop and enhance one's skill set. The acquisition of these novel and invaluable skills will have a positive influence on various aspects of your life.

INSTANCES OF SUPPLEMENTARY INCOME SOURCES

Listed herein, are several examples of supplementary endeavors that you may consider exploring with the intention of enhancing your financial advancement.

OFFERING TUTORING SERVICES

Providing tutoring services proves to be a highly advantageous opportunity, as numerous children have a strong inclination towards seeking supplementary academic assistance for their studies. Individually, you have the option to offer your services either through personal interaction or make them accessible online. Additionally, it is important to acknowledge the fulfillment one derives from assisting students.

CARING FOR A DOMESTIC ANIMAL

Certain pet owners require this service in order to ensure the proper care of their pets when they are away from home or occupied with work. It is imperative to have a genuine affection for animals prior to contemplating this pursuit as an additional source of income.

PURSUING A CAREER AS A MUSIC EDUCATOR

This opportunity is equally splendid if you possess expertise in music or have proficiency in playing a musical instrument. This service is conveniently accessible from the comfort of your own residence, or alternatively, from a reputable music venue.

EMBARKING ON A CAREER AS A FOOD DELIVERY SPECIALIST

For the purpose of this supplementary employment opportunity, it is expected that you undertake the responsibility of conveying food orders from participating eateries to the designated residential and commercial addresses as specified by the customers. This additional business opportunity may afford you the flexibility to offer food delivery services during the entire operating hours of the establishment.

BECOMING A CAREGIVER

This particular type of supplementary employment allows individuals to render caregiving services to children, elderly individuals, individuals afflicted with illnesses, or those suffering from injuries. This service is available for delivery at both clients' residences and caregiving facilities.

BECOMING A CLEANER

This particular supplementary occupation incorporates a diverse range of opportunities, encompassing the maintenance and tidying of private residences, commercial establishments, and automobiles.

You also have the opportunity to pursue a career as a professional landscaper.
This opportunity has the potential to be a supplementary source of income due to the fact that a large number of households possess lawns that require upkeep, thereby increasing the likelihood of acquiring numerous prospective customers. This service is available both within your local neighborhood and in other areas.

Embarking on a Career as a Fitness Instructor
This additional professional pursuit offers you the chance to assist individuals in achieving their fitness objectives, while simultaneously instilling a sense of personal gratification. This service can be made available at a public gym, or alternatively at a park or within your private facility, should you possess one. Possessing specific licenses and

certifications may be necessary in order to pursue this supplementary endeavor.

BECOMING A TAILOR

Acquiring skills in tailoring and sewing can offer you the opportunity to establish a supplementary source of income. This task will require you to make modifications that are tailored to accommodate the specific physique of your client. Modifications can be made to wedding attire, as well as any garments that are presented to you. With this supplementary employment opportunity, you can attract a multitude of clients who are enthusiastically seeking your services.

There exists a wide array of supplementary sources of income to partake in, many of which are not exhaustively covered within this chapter. However, if you genuinely desire to augment your earnings, it would be prudent to take immediate action. What is deterring you from doing so? It is now time to commence the activities.

7 Effective Strategies for Enhancing Your Financial Management Skills

These suggestions for money management have the potential to establish a foundation for sustained financial prosperity and enhance your ability to handle finances more proficiently.

If financial concerns are a stressor in your life, rest assured that you are not alone. The findings of the 2020 Capital One Mind Over Money Study demonstrated that a significant proportion of the participants, precisely 77%, expressed apprehension regarding their financial situations.

Presented below are several actionable measures that can be pursued immediately to enhance your confidence and optimize your financial management skills.

Key Takeaways:

When one adopts an intelligent and effective approach to the management of wealth and the planning of finances, it can pave the way for a promising and prosperous future.

Effective Financial Administration Encompasses More than Mere Budgeting.

There exist two empirically validated approaches aimed at aiding individuals in effectively managing and repaying their debt.

What Is Money Management?

Financial management encompasses activities such as budgeting, investing, saving, and expenditure. Thus, what strategies can be implemented to cultivate a sense of financial self-assurance and alleviate concerns pertaining to one's financial objectives? Discovering alternative strategies to effectively handle your finances, while also nurturing a positive mentality, has the potential to be advantageous. You may consider conducting independent research or seeking expert advice to aid you in formulating your financial plan.

Strategies for Enhancing Money Management Skills

Consider utilizing these seven practical financial tips and acquiring effective money management skills as a comprehensive reference to steer your financial endeavors.

1. Create a personalized financial plan

The Capital One Mind Over Money Study has revealed that individuals who are experiencing the effects of financial stress encounter greater difficulties in managing their budgets. They experience a reduced sense of agency and are inclined to exhibit more impulsive spending behaviors when handling their wages.

Crafting a budget serves as an effective initial measure in cultivating more prudent financial behaviors and acquiring the skills to maximize the utilization of your financial resources.

As per the findings of the Consumer Financial Protection Bureau (CFPB), proper budgeting is integral to ensuring a sufficient allocation of funds towards both essential and desired expenditures, while simultaneously fostering the growth of savings to meet future aspirations.

You may commence by employing a budgeting worksheet and adhering to the prescribed procedural measures such as the following:

Calculate your monthly earnings. This encompasses your remuneration from your occupation, as well as additional avenues of income such as supplementary earnings, tax reimbursements, or proceeds from incidental employment.

Calculate Your Monthly Expenditures. These may encompass expenditures classified under significant categories such as housing payments, food expenses, student loan repayments, and transportation costs. In instances where the monthly payments vary, such as those for food and utilities, an alternative approach would be to calculate an average based on the previous months' expenditures.

Deduct Your Expenditures from Your Earnings. This sum will serve as the initial point for your budget. The residual amount is what remains at your disposal for debt repayment and savings accumulation. If the remaining amount is insufficient, it may be prudent to contemplate cost reduction measures for expenditures such as takeout meals and subscriptions, if such action has not already been taken.

Considering your budget as a dynamic document subject to frequent review can be beneficial. By following this approach, you will have the flexibility to make necessary modifications, such as the elimination of a recurring expenditure by settling a credit card debt. When devising your budget, it may be worth considering alternative budgeting methodologies that are commonly employed, such as the widely recognized 50/30/20 rule.

2. Track Your Spending

According to the Capital One Mind Over Money Study, implementing prudent financial practices during times of financial security can prove beneficial when faced with more demanding circumstances.

Maintaining meticulous records of your expenditures has the potential to become a commendable practice. Ultimately, it may assist you in mitigating excessive expenditure and adhering to your budget.

What methods do you employ to monitor your expenditure? It's Simple. One can consider utilizing the plethora of available digital applications online to record their expenses.

If you possess a Capital One card, you may avail yourself of the complimentary digital functionalities designed to assist you in monitoring your financial transactions. Alternatively, should you have a preference for a paper-based solution, you may opt to retain your receipts and meticulously document all transactions within a planner or notebook.

One practical suggestion is to consider organizing your expenses by category for better clarity and organization. By doing so, you will gain insight into the allocation of your funds and identify potential areas of excessive expenditure.

3. Save For Retirement

Unsurprisingly, the findings of the Capital One Mind Over Money study revealed that Americans harbor concerns regarding their financial prospects. This entails setting aside funds for one's retirement. Additionally, it was revealed that a significant percentage of respondents, precisely 68%, expressed concerns regarding their future financial stability in retirement.

It could be beneficial to commence with modest contributions towards retirement savings. To rephrase the statement in a formal tone: "To clarify, you have the option to allocate a modest sum each month for the time being, and subsequently augment it at your discretion."

It can be advantageous to consider establishing a retirement plan account that can serve as an additional source of income to complement retirement benefits derived from pensions or social security. The following categories of accounts may encompass the following varieties:

Employer-Sponsored 401(K) Retirement Plan. Through a regular deduction from your paycheck, you have the ability to deposit pre-tax dollars into your 401(K) account. According to Beth Sabin, a high-ranking executive at Capital One, initiating contributions to your 401(K) plan, especially if your company offers a matching program, can serve as an advantageous initial step. Not only does she suggest fully capitalizing on this matching opportunity, but she also proposes experimenting with a modest 1% increase in contribution to evaluate its feasibility for your financial circumstances. In the event that it is so, you may consider augmenting it by an additional percentage point in order to expedite the growth of your savings.

403(B) Plan. Similar to 401(k) plans, 403(b) plans are employer-sponsored. A distinction can be observed whereby 403(B) plans are provided by public educational institutions and certain tax-exempt organizations. Contributions made to traditional 403(b) plans are subject to tax deferral, similar to traditional 401(k) plans. Hence, no tax obligations are incurred in relation to the contributions or earnings until such time as the funds are withdrawn from the account.

Individual Retirement Account (IRA). Deposits made towards a Traditional IRA, which is usually managed by the account holder and not administered by an employer, enjoy the benefit of tax deferral. Upon reaching retirement and commencing withdrawals, the funds will be subject to taxation at the prevailing rate of your personal income tax.

Roth IRA. Although there are no tax deductions for contributions made to a Roth IRA, it is possible to potentially enjoy tax-free withdrawal of funds during your retirement phase.

It is advisable to seek guidance from your tax adviser for further details regarding these plans.

Please be mindful that the phenomenon of compound interest has the potential to serve as a significant incentive for initiating savings at an early stage. According to the Consumer Financial Protection Bureau's elucidation, the phenomenon of compound interest has the potential to expedite the growth of your savings by generating interest on accrued interest. To comprehend the cumulative impact of compound interest, it is recommended that you make use of the compound interest calculator provided by the U.S. Securities and Exchange Commission.

4. Save For Emergencies

Accumulating funds in a contingency fund for unforeseen life circumstances, such as encountering substantial home maintenance expenses, can potentially enhance your sense of financial security.

Expanding your savings may be among your objectives. "If such a circumstance arises, you might find it prudent to deliberate on the following financial suggestions in order to address unforeseen expenditures:

Please be advised that interest rates have the potential to differ. Therefore, it is advisable to explore different options before making a decision. If one discovers a savings account offering a more advantageous interest rate, the incremental interest earned can accumulate significantly over a period of time.

Deposit Supplementary Earnings Into Your Account. When receiving a tax refund or a bonus from your employment, it would be prudent to contemplate placing these funds into your bank account. The additional funds can contribute to the growth of your savings.

Prioritize Purchasing Necessities Over Desires. In this manner, you can allocate the remainder towards your savings.

Set Up Automatic Savings. With the assistance of your employer, it is possible to establish automated transfers to your savings account in order to cultivate your savings without succumbing to the temptation of excessive expenditure.

5. Debt Repayment Strategy

The repayment of debt can also facilitate enhanced financial management and alleviate anxiety pertaining to monetary matters.

The following are two strategies suggested by the Consumer Financial Protection Bureau (CFPB) to achieve financial independence from debt:

The Snowball Method entails prioritizing the repayment of your smallest balances as a key focus. You continue to fulfill the minimum payment requirements for all of your outstanding debts. Simultaneously, any surplus funds are allocated towards the settlement of your lowest outstanding balance. Subsequently, you utilize the funds you have liberated to settle your subsequent-smallest balance and continue the process iteratively. Consequently, debts bearing higher interest rates may ultimately necessitate a longer time to be fully repaid. In the long term, this could result in higher costs for you.

Debt Avalanche Method: Employing this approach, commonly known as the Highest-Interest-Rate Method, involves organizing your debts in descending order based on their respective interest rates. You should allocate your funds towards the debt that carries the highest interest rate initially. After the previous payment has been settled, you can allocate the surplus funds towards the subsequent loan on your agenda. You consistently adhere to making the minimum payments on all of your debts as well.

6. Develop and cultivate a positive credit behavior

Striving towards the cultivation of favorable credit scores may additionally enhance your financial well-being.

Based on the information provided by the CFPB, your credit scores serve as a depiction of your creditworthiness. Consequently, these scores have the potential to influence various aspects of your life, ranging from securing a rental agreement to being evaluated as a potential candidate for employment opportunities.

The Consumer Financial Protection Bureau (CFPB) advises incorporating the following measures into an individual's personal finance management strategy in order to establish a commendable credit record:

Ensure prompt and timely settlement of your financial obligations, without fail, on a monthly basis.

Do not approach the maximum thresholds on your credit accounts.

Focus on developing an extensive credit history.

Consistently monitoring your credit reports for precision can also prove beneficial. Creditwise, offered by Capital One, provides a convenient method for monitoring your Vantagescore® 3.0 credit score and Transunion® credit report. It will not have any detrimental impact on your credit scores. It is available to all individuals, regardless of whether they are using a Capital One product, and there are no charges for its usage. Additionally, it is possible to obtain complimentary copies of your credit reports from each of the three prominent credit bureaus by visiting the website annualcreditreport.com.

As you strive towards achieving your financial objectives, it may be prudent to contemplate how integrating a Capital One credit card into your financial strategy could be advantageous. By exercising responsible utilization, you have the potential to leverage a credit card to either establish or rehabilitate your credit score, thereby enhancing your financial trajectory.

7. Enhance Your Financial Mindset.

The manner in which you allocate your financial resources carries significant weight. However, the perspective you hold regarding the matter also bears significance.

Adopting a more optimistic financial perspective during fiscal management may involve maintaining focus on your objectives. Alternatively, it may entail adopting a solution-driven mindset and directing your attention towards factors that are within your control, such as the repayment of your financial obligations and the management of your expenditure patterns.

For further insights into these and other strategies for effective personal financial management, we encourage you to refer to the comprehensive findings of the Capital One Mind Over Money Study.

Please be aware that if you are experiencing stress regarding the management of your finances, handling personal monetary matters, or achieving your savings objectives, it is important to understand that you are not the only one. Now that you have acquired additional knowledge on methods for financial management, including the principles of budgeting, debt repayment, and the establishment of an emergency fund. With persistent effort, those actions may eventually develop into habitual behaviors. This can potentially pave the way for financial prosperity at all stages of your life.

The majority of individuals frequently engage in discussions pertaining to increasing their financial earnings; however, only a limited number of people address the subject of effectively managing these funds. While the acquisition of wealth is crucial, it is of equal significance to safeguard and employ one's financial resources judiciously. It is imperative to exercise prudence in preserving, allocating, and utilizing your diligently acquired financial resources in a methodical fashion, so as to secure enduring stability and adequate fluidity in the long run. This can be achieved by implementing efficient financial management techniques.

An Important Aspect Of Money Management Is Keeping A Track Of Your Expenses And Reviewing Them Periodically. This facilitates the maintenance of financial control. It aids in the identification and reduction of superfluous expenditures, while prioritizing essential expenditures.

Presented below are several strategies for effectively managing your finances:

1. Create A Budget:

Developing a financial plan is the initial and paramount measure of effective fiscal management. It is a relatively straightforward method that has been employed for centuries. To construct a budget, it is advisable to assess and determine the projected monthly expenses by considering your income, lifestyle, and desired expenditures. Acquiring such an approximation will facilitate the attainment of greater financial management, thereby enabling the systematic arrangement of your expenditures and savings. By exercising greater control and cultivating a heightened awareness of your expenditures, you will be empowered to monitor and attain your financial objectives with utmost efficacy, all while upholding your desired standard of living.

2. Prioritize Saving Over Spending:

As a general guideline, it is advisable to set aside a portion of your monthly earnings prior to allocating funds for essential expenditures such as groceries, rent, electricity, loan installments, insurance premiums, and the like. This guarantees your preparedness for any potential future circumstances, thereby mitigating the risk of overspending or surpassing your budget.

3. Set Financial Goals:

Establishing a financial objective enables one to maintain concentration and prevent excessive expenditure. Thus, devise a comprehensive strategy for managing your financial resources both in the immediate and distant future. To attain your envisioned objectives for the future, such as owning your desired residence, ensuring your child's education, securing a comfortable retirement, and more, it is imperative to commence investing in diverse financial instruments. It is important to consistently establish achievable objectives coupled with defined timeframes. This will aid in maintaining your motivation and ensuring prudent allocation of your financial resources.

4. Start Investing Early:

It is highly recommended to initiate the practice of saving money at the earliest feasible stage of one's life. This affords you an increased opportunity to cultivate your wealth and yield greater returns in the long term. Consequently, endeavor to commence budgeting and allocating funds into investments as soon as you receive your initial salary. ICICI Pru Lifetime Classic1 serves as an excellent vehicle for the accumulation of wealth over an extended period, making it an optimal choice for individuals seeking long-term savings. This Unit Linked Plan2 provides dual advantages, including safeguarding the financial interests of your loved ones through a life cover^, and also creating substantial funds to achieve your financial objectives. The plan provides four different portfolio strategies, allowing individuals to select any of these options based on their specific objectives and tolerance for risk. You Can Choose Between Equity, Balance, And Debt Funds, And Switch Between These Funds At Any Point In Time, Without Any Additional Charges. Furthermore, the aforementioned scheme offers the opportunity to obtain loyalty additions3 and wealth boosters4 as a means of recognition for maintaining your investment for an extended duration and consistently making premium payments without any lapses. This significantly contributes to your overall income. Additionally, you have the option to make monthly, semi-annual, or annual premium payments, or you may opt for a single lump-sum payment. In addition, you are entitled to tax advantages of up to ₹ 46,800/- on the premiums paid, as per the provisions of Section 80C of the Income Tax Act, 1961.

5. Avoid Debt:

Although obtaining loans in order to pursue personal aspirations is a prevalent approach, it is essential to acknowledge that they are not without their challenges. The substantial interest charges can erode your savings. Assuming multiple loans also has an impact on your credit score, thus rendering it more challenging to obtain credit when absolutely essential or, in certain scenarios, even employment opportunities. Therefore, endeavor to minimize your debt to the greatest extent feasible. Relying heavily on credit cards or accumulating excessive debt has the potential to adversely affect your financial circumstances, impeding your budget and imposing a significant financial burden.

How To Increase Your Wealth While Safeguarding Every Euro

Augment Your Financial Assets While Preventing Any Loss of Euro... Is it truly achievable?

Perhaps I have been fortunate, but I have been engaged in investment activities for a period exceeding 20 years. Admittedly, I made a series of early errors, but once I comprehended the necessary steps for achieving success as an investor, I implemented them consistently. The fluctuations witnessed in the real estate market, the notable instances of large-scale financial frauds, or the economic phenomena characterized by rapid expansion and subsequent collapse that have led to financial losses and immense distress among numerous individuals... Have not made the slightest physical contact with me.

This has had a significant impact over the course of time as it has enabled me to consistently augment my financial assets year after year, without encountering any instances of financial loss in any given year.

Soon after initiation, I engaged in numerous instructional sessions, during which I consistently gained substantial knowledge unlike the majority of participants. I acquired knowledge regarding these occurrences, along with strategies to evade the errors that individuals typically encounter, and oftentimes, repeat on multiple occasions throughout their lifetime. Errors that Hinder the Accumulation of Wealth.

Regrettably, the typical investor's financial journey is marked by an abundance of endeavors to speculate, driven by the optimism that circumstances will align favorably. Only a small minority are able to attain fulfillment in their aspirations. Regrettably, there exists a considerable number of individuals who experience significant financial losses.

Although my track record as an investor may not be particularly thrilling, it has undeniably been more lucrative. It is essential to consider this factor if you aspire to enhance your financial resources.

I adhere to prevailing trends in investment, entering into positions only when indicators of growth and sustained progress are evident, and promptly divesting when these criteria are no longer upheld. This frequently inclines me to decline opportunities that do not progress in accordance with my preferred trajectory.

For instance, I actively participated in the recent surge of the real estate market in Italy, reaping numerous advantages. However, when prices escalated to levels surpassing 20 times the potential annual rental value, I unequivocally discerned that it was prudent to exit the market.

When I refrained from making purchases and counseled others to exercise caution, unless prices were deemed reasonable, an individual perceived my behavior as eccentric due to the market's persistence at its highest point. Now, there are still those who remind me of the accuracy of my previous statements ...

I am conveying this information not with the intention of boasting, but to prompt your contemplation on an essential matter: One can exercise prudence in investments without necessitating a sophisticated level of investor expertise.

It can be accomplished simply by assessing numerical values and employing a minimal amount of rational thinking.

Maximize Your Financial Growth, While Mitigating Risk: 5 Key Errors to Steer Clear of

Engage in the Captivating Narratives

I retain a particularly vivid recollection of a remarkable tale that transpired several years in the past. Unconventional Events, Derived from the World of Hollywood.

Movie ...

The narrative revolves around a United States-based corporation engaged in the extraction of gold from a sandy coastline situated within a region of Central America. I am aware that it may appear quite astonishing today, however, during that period...

The Company presented compelling substantiation, including an audited balance sheet, findings from numerous geologists, and assessments from multiple investment professionals.

The individuals who provided me with this information at that time had personally visited the location to confirm the veracity of these claims, and they witnessed the remarkable spectacle of sand being introduced into a machinery, resulting in the production of gold dust.

I refrained from investing in that initiative, despite the numerous promises and compelling evidence and testimonials presented, due to the excessively captivating nature of the narrative, which strongly evoked the notion of alchemical utopia. In any event, my knowledge and understanding of geology or gold at that time were limited, but it was the overwhelming emotional response elicited by the history that raised my suspicions.

Individuals ceased to evaluate investment opportunities and instead pursued the fulfillment of an unattainable aspiration.

Ever since that point in time, whenever I come across such narratives or when confronted with any investment proposition that relies primarily on sentiments rather than concrete agreements, I have remained entirely cautious.

One portion of my cognitive faculty might be inclined towards enthusiasm, however, the more logical compartment promptly advises me to exercise caution and maintain distance. A prosperous investor consistently pays heed to this hearsay.

Engaging in an investment in which they lack knowledge and understanding.

The individual mentioned previously had the characteristics and investment knowledge associated with a sophisticated investor. He possessed a profound understanding of stock market investment strategies, demonstrating expertise in both fundamental analysis and technical analysis. Given the circumstances, he was undeniably regarded as a prosperous investor in this particular context.

Notwithstanding these remarks, his knowledge in regards to industrial production, geology, mining, or gold mining remained insufficient. Due to his lack of knowledge, he was susceptible to being misled by the reports provided to him and by visiting a facility that ultimately did not exist.

The aforementioned fraudulent scheme remained confined to the mining sector, as its perpetrators were fully aware that competent individuals within the industry would promptly discern the meticulously forged nature of the operation, thus rendering it inconsequential.

If one possesses no comprehension of the subject matter in which they are allocating their funds, they resemble an individual devoid of sight who endeavors to traverse a congested thoroughfare during peak traffic hours. Have I grasped the concept?

It could potentially be acceptable for you ... What is the probability of this occurrence?

Being the preferred targets of disingenuous companions and adept manipulators.

As previously stated, I also made erroneous investment decisions, one example being during the early stages of my venture in the real estate industry. The errors arose due to a convergence of the initial two factors mentioned, but most significantly due to yielding to the influence exerted by a skilled real estate broker, who I also held in high regard as a trusted acquaintance.

I consented to undertaking those investments, despite a prevailing intuition suggesting their potential failure. I disregarded my intuition due to his adeptness at leveraging my emotional faculties, particularly those associated with a driven and aspiring individual fervently seeking rapid advancement.

It is possible that these experiences have played a significant role in shaping me into a highly proficient salesperson. This influence has been so profound that I have garnered recognition as a respected instructor in sales leadership. My distinctive quality lies in my capacity to impart effective sales techniques while upholding principles of honesty and ethics.

Engaging in late-stage market investments

In spite of the initial errors, I have subsequently negotiated lucrative transactions in the real estate industry over the course of several years. It occurred during a period of price escalation, especially when you made purchases at exceptionally favorable values. This enabled me to generate substantial earnings when prices experienced rapid escalation.

Nevertheless, as previously indicated, upon realizing that it was no longer feasible to effortlessly acquire properties at valuations equivalent to 8 or 10 times their annual rental income, I made a conscious decision to curtail my investments in order to optimize my profits upon exiting the market.

What is the appropriate moment to depart? When inexperienced investors start to appear, those who enter a sector solely due to its popularity, thus contributing to a complete market bubble. That's The Time To Get Out Because The Bubble Will Burst Shortly Thereafter.

If you arrive tardily, indeed, the sole opportunity to garner profits from your investments lies in encountering an individual of deranged disposition who enters at an even more misguided moment, an individual who possesses even lesser understanding of the said market than yourself. However, in the event of this game's failure, there is a significant financial risk at stake for you.

It would seem that individuals possessing even a basic level of prudence would abstain from succumbing to the inclination to enter a market by investing at the most unfavorable juncture. Regrettably, a multitude of Italians, comprising both financial institutions and brokers, have indeed done so.

There exists a moment to embark upon a market venture and a moment to withdraw. Both of these entities can be readily identified if one directs their attention towards the underlying principles of any economic cycle, instead of succumbing to the emotional fervor typically associated with speculative bubbles.

Engaging in Investment Activities without Implementing Risk Mitigation Measures

Even if one exercises rational thinking and refrains from committing the aforementioned four errors, there is still potential to incur financial losses as a result of unforeseen circumstances.

In order to mitigate this risk, it is imperative to abide by a single principle: refrain from making any investments that do not offer a viable exit strategy. It is not solely pertinent to the stock market, but it also extends its relevance to any entrepreneurial endeavor.

What provisions are outlined in the contract/agreement that offer an avenue for resolution or termination?

Resuming activities in the real estate sector ... An alternative expression in a formal tone could be: "One possible solution could be the potential revenue generated through the rental of the property, in case selling it is not a viable option due to various circumstances."

When engaging in stock market investments, the potential avenues for exiting such positions comprise the implementation of either a stop loss order or a trailing stop order.

Alternatively, one may also consider the income generated from the ownership of shares in the form of dividends. You Are There?

Below are five prevalent errors committed by the general investor population. Those who impede the expansion of your financial prosperity. As evident from the aforementioned, nevertheless, all of these can be mitigated through prudent and astute action.

Please take a moment to reflect upon your past investment experiences and the current investments you are considering. Promptly inquire within yourself: "Have I committed or am I presently committing any of these five errors?"

Pose the query to oneself, and then adopt a course of action consistent with the response, as sidestepping these errors will afford the opportunity to preserve capital and augment financial resources.

1. Do not shy away from addressing matters pertaining to finances in the presence of your children, be it during mealtime, while running errands, or during car rides. Engage in open discussions about certain financial choices you make in order to involve your children in these matters. This serves a dual purpose: firstly, it facilitates the acquisition of financial literacy skills by your children, and secondly, it compels you to assume responsibility for your financial management. You will discover yourself assuming greater financial responsibility through engaging in conversations about finances in the presence of your children.

2. Utilize Significant Achievements as an Educational Opportunity for Your Children: When they secure their initial employment, engage in a thoughtful dialogue about effective financial management. If you secure a new employment opportunity, please ensure

to include it in the conversation. One could express a statement such as "I have secured employment that offers a higher income." I intend to allocate the additional funds I am earning towards settling my credit card debts, with the purpose of improving my credit score."

3. Providing a financial allocation offers a valuable opportunity to educate children in matters of fiscal responsibility, provided that consistency is maintained. Additionally, it may be advantageous to incentivize positive behavior by periodically granting salary increases commensurate with the satisfactory completion of assigned household tasks or scholastic achievements. View yourself as the overseer of your child's activities and responsibilities. Monitor their financial activities closely. If individuals are making an effort to purchase unhealthy food, it presents a valuable opportunity for imparting knowledge and guidance.

Good day, I am Abigail. I was indeed born in South Carolina; however, my current place of residence is Cleveland, Ohio, where I reside with my spouse and two children. Presently, life is quite magnificent. We are nearing the completion of our mortgage payments, which is a significant milestone. Additionally, our children are enrolled in an exceptional local school, while both my spouse and I are fortunate to have fulfilling professional careers. Furthermore, all family members enjoy sound physical well-being. We possess many reasons to express gratitude.

Indeed, a mere year ago we were not bestowed with fortune. Our financial situation was in disarray. I was unable to make timely bill payments, and as a result, our creditors began contacting us. However, we still had to allocate resources for our sustenance. It is rather peculiar how these financial challenges gradually manifest, don't you agree? Certainly, during my time in college, I had the privilege of being awarded a scholarship, which I consider myself fortunate to have received. My part-time employment provided adequate compensation for both accommodation and sustenance, allowing me to retain a modest surplus that permitted me to enjoy occasional social outings with friends and indulge in limited travel experiences.

However, upon entering into matrimony, I was unfortunately met with the onset of the economic downturn. My spouse faced unemployment, while I was unable to seek employment due to my pregnancy. When we became parents to both children, we encountered significant financial challenges. Times Were Tough. On a certain occasion, my daughter Tina apprised me of her requirement for new footwear to participate in the cheerleading team. I experienced a profound sense of distress, yet regrettably, I was compelled to decline due to our insufficiency of financial resources. Finally, a catalyst emerged that facilitated our transformation.

We were able to achieve substantial monthly savings only after we began diligently employing coupon-clipping techniques. Furthermore, apart from my part-time employment, a considerable portion of my time is devoted to diligently cutting out and organizing coupons. The Great Thing? I have great affection for this activity. It provides me the opportunity to either accompany the children or indulge in watching my preferred film, all while engaging in the task of trimming coupons and strategically planning our monthly food budget allocation. I possess proficient skills in the art of 'couponing,' which consistently enables us to achieve noteworthy savings of at least 100 dollars during each of our shopping trips. We currently possess all the necessary provisions, thus ensuring our daily sustenance with consistently nutritious meals. Coupons have proven to be a valuable financial resource for both myself and my family. "

:: :: ::

Utilizing coupons for purchases you typically make can prove to be economically advantageous, as it allows for potential monetary savings. However, it is important to bear in mind that the financial benefits of coupon clipping are contingent upon using these coupons for the purchase of your regular items. If one were to utilize a coupon to purchase an item that is not necessarily essential, it would be considered a frivolous expenditure of funds.

As an illustration, if one were to purchase paper towels on a monthly basis and happen to receive a coupon in the amount of $1 off during the current month, this would prove advantageous as it would result in a reduction of $1 from the total grocery expenditure. However, should you opt to utilize a coupon this month in order to acquire the hair brush that is currently discounted, it would be deemed an unnecessary expenditure. If you were to purchase the items that you commonly buy, such as paper towels, the cumulative expenditure would exceed your usual spending even after considering the discount provided by the coupon.

That scenario presented is rudimentary in nature. However, envision the implications if one were to consistently apply this approach across a diverse array of products. If one is able to appropriately utilize coupons for their routine purchases and manage to adhere to their budget, it can be asserted that they are essentially acquiring additional monetary resources at no cost through coupon clipping.

Greetings, my name is William and I currently reside in Minneapolis, Minnesota. I am currently 45 years of age, engaged in a professional occupation within the realm of education. Throughout the course of time, I have come to realize that it is an inevitable necessity for individuals to diligently oversee their financial affairs in order to ensure sustenance. At present, you may perhaps be harboring the thought that the insight I have shared is widely known, and indeed, you are correct in your observation. Nonetheless, it is worth noting that a considerable number of individuals fail to comprehend the profound significance of money in relation to their very existence and livelihood. If such were the case, they would exhibit greater accountability in managing their financial matters.

Let Me Explain. In my adolescent phase when I embarked on my initial professional journey, I was not provided with any guidance on financial management. Similar to the majority of individuals, upon receiving my paycheck, I unconsciously expended the funds without considering the future. As long as I made purchases within my desired range and adhered to my financial capacity, prioritizing financial responsibility was deemed insignificant.

Also, Strange As This Might Sound, Saving Money Just Did Not Make Sense To Me Either. In the past, I naively harbored the belief that possessing true masculinity entailed managing my finances independently without the necessity of a bank account. Are you able to perceive the imprudence of my thought process? Thank God It Changed.

During that period, I relied on my monthly salary to make ends meet. I operated under the assumption that my weekly wages were guaranteed, prompting me to exhaust the entirety of my available funds. Once again, I displayed my lack of knowledge. This is the consequence that ensues when one remains uninformed about the significance of saving and lacks proper guidance on constraining expenditure.

Over time, I ultimately resigned from a significant number of positions I held during my adolescent years due to my persistent belief in securing alternative employment opportunities. The cultivation of such a detrimental practice proved highly disadvantageous as it inhibited the acquisition of necessary skills for sustaining employment. Sustaining employment is crucial for an individual's financial well-being, as the absence of gainful employment renders the acquisition of income exceedingly challenging.

Only in my mid-30s did I truly grasp the significance of prudent saving and spending. At the time, all four of my children were in their early years, necessitating that I devise a plan to effectively provide for their needs.

I continue to encounter occasional financial challenges despite earning an annual income of approximately $50,000. I'm Not Rich. Particularly when it entails the responsibility of nourishing, clothing, and catering for four children. Being entrusted with the responsibility of others can accelerate your personal growth at a rapid pace. It will also compel you to swiftly acquire the knowledge and skills required for proficiently overseeing your personal financial matters.

I strongly advocate for the commitment of all young individuals to maintain stable employment. Do not resign from your position unless you have successfully secured employment with another organization. Save Your Money.

It is not necessary to save all of it, but it is advisable to set aside a portion. In adherence to Christian principles, it is expected that believers commit to tithing. Allocate your financial resources towards essential expenditures such as fuel, housing, food provisions, and utility payments. Exercise restraint in allocating your financial resources towards the acquisition of video games, CDs, clothing, mobile devices, cigarettes, alcoholic beverages, illicit substances, magazines, and various other non-essential items.

It is imperative to exercise prudent fiscal management from an early age in regard to your personal finances. If one is able to grasp this principle at an early stage, they will lead a life with greater financial rewards. This principle can be implemented by individuals of advanced age as well, as it is a timeless truth that one can always initiate change, regardless of their stage in life. That's All I Got."

:: :: ::

Engaging in early financial savings can yield substantial advantages in the future. I would like to draw attention to the notion of "quality of life," which can be enhanced through gradual savings. Consider the sequence of occurrences that transpire when one reaches adulthood and lacks financial resources. We experience stress due to financial constraints, which leads us to seek solace in indulgent activities or food (leading to weight gain and related concerns). Consequently, stress manifests in various ways, causing personal or familial challenges that permeate nearly every facet of our lives.

By commencing saving at an early stage (or beginning promptly), with potentially several decades ahead, and adopting a lifestyle of frugality, a significant proportion of those concerns can be alleviated. The significant reduction in financial capability is deeply alleviated.

Throughout my years as an adult, I have consistently encountered financial indebtedness. I am Mary, a resident of Monroe County, Pennsylvania. Priorly, I pursued a full-time occupation, however, the financial resources at my disposal proved to be insufficient. I possessed merely a pair of credit cards. One that I made a purchase with, while the other was reserved solely for emergency situations. I was unable to ascertain the underlying reasons for the substantial debt I had incurred and the factors contributing to my financial mismanagement. I was enlightened by an acquaintance who recommended the book titled "How To Attain Financial

Freedom, Sustain It, and Thrive," which draws its principles from the esteemed Debtors Anonymous Program. After perusing this literary piece, I assimilated several insights that aided me in restoring focus and initiating the process of overcoming my financial liabilities.

This book has provided me with valuable insights into the factors that have contributed to my financial indebtedness. One initial error that I made was my lack of awareness regarding the actual balance present in my checking account. I possessed a rough approximation, yet remained unaware of the precise quantity. I opted for online banking with the intention of monitoring the deductions made from my account and maintaining a real-time understanding of my balance. Another error I committed was frequently resorting to seeking financial assistance from acquaintances and relatives. I would refrain from borrowing a substantial sum. As I do not possess physical currency, I relied on the generosity of others each time we made a stop for fast food, as they kindly covered the small sum of money I owed. Over a substantial period of time, this accumulated sum of money. Consequently, I found myself indebted to friends and family with a significantly higher amount of money than originally anticipated. I, too, had inadequacies in my savings practices. My employer deducts funds for my 401K directly from my paycheck. I currently lack a savings account or any additional funds allocated for unforeseen circumstances when solely dependent on my own resources.

I had the desire to undergo transformation, yet remained unaware of the means to achieve such. This publication offered me insightful strategies for gradually overcoming financial indebtedness. It may appear self-evident, nonetheless, my primary course of action necessitated ceasing the accumulation of additional debt. I have begun to adopt the habit of leaving my credit cards behind at home, opting instead to visit my bank in order to withdraw a modest sum of cash. I filled up my car with gasoline for the entire week and procured groceries. Subsequently, in the event that my funds were depleted, I refrained from indulging in unnecessary purchases. This prevented me from further accruing charges on my credit card. I implemented the recommendation to maintain a record of my earnings. I commenced by utilizing my subsequent salary to meticulously record the net amount of funds received after tax deductions. I subsequently proceeded to subtract all of my expenses, including my mid-afternoon coffee, from my total. This permitted me to ascertain the areas where my financial resources were being allocated and identify the areas where modifications were required.

This book has served as a catalyst for me, enabling me to gain a profound understanding of the financial adjustments I needed to make. While I am still in debt, I am exerting considerable effort to ensure that I remain up-to-date with all of my financial obligations and refrain from accruing additional debt that could prove overwhelming."

In my own experience, this book had a profound impact on the way I handle and manage my finances. I experienced a perpetual state of inebriation with regards to my expenses, akin to that of an individual labeled as an alcoholic. I Couldn't Stop. This literary work facilitated a shift in my perception, enabling me to gain a broader and more comprehensive understanding of various aspects. Please direct your attention to one of the subheadings within the chapter, as it contains all the essential information required.

The Unremitted Payment; Insufficient Initial Payment; Borrowed Funds; Has the 15th of the month arrived?; The Imbalanced Financial Statement.

It addresses nearly all of the concerns encountered by individuals grappling with financial matters, particularly those pertaining to wealth accumulation and indebtedness. I do not possess the role of the publisher or author of the book; however, it provided immense assistance to me.

I am Mary, and my place of residence is located in East Stroudsburg, Pennsylvania. I possess a respectable occupation, yet inexplicably I find myself facing financial constraints. It was a source of great frustration that I dedicated an entire week to my work endeavors, yet had no tangible outcomes to showcase. I was well aware that it was imperative for me to devise a solution to this predicament.

My initial action entailed enrolling in online banking services provided by my financial institution. In this manner, I could ascertain the exact amount of funds in my account at any given moment. Additionally, I observed that the payment for my car insurance was being automatically debited from my bank account. Surprisingly, I was not aware of this fact, resulting in excessive expenditures on my part. Essentially, I failed to monitor my income and expenditures adequately.

I have additionally made the decision to construct a financial plan. I was aware of the precise amount of money I had to allocate towards monthly rent, as well as my car payment and car insurance expenses. I calculated the average cost of my electric, cable, and cell phone bills. Upon reviewing these invoices, I have opted to eliminate some of the supplementary channels from my cable subscription in order to reduce costs. I formulate a financial plan to determine the appropriate weekly allocation for food expenses. Additionally, I allocated a designated amount of funds for my personal amusement. This would encompass dining at restaurants, indulging in beverages at establishments, renting movies, as well as the fuel consumption required to travel to visit friends at their residences. In addition, I have taken into account the weekly allocation needed for transportation expenses towards commuting to my workplace. I allocated a modest sum of money in my budget specifically for the purpose of depositing it into a savings account. During that period, I had a weekly allowance of only $10 to allocate towards my savings, although I recognized that any amount was better than none. In the event of an unforeseen circumstance such as a car repair or any other type of emergency, having a small sum of money set aside would significantly enhance my state of preparedness.

Although I do not possess great wealth, I am now more financially stable and no longer endure periods of financial hardship. All of my financial obligations have been met, allowing me the opportunity to enjoy leisure activities without concern. Crafting an Authentic Budget has been the most advantageous measure I have taken to improve my financial circumstances. I would also like to emphasize the utmost significance of closely monitoring your expenses and savings on a continuous basis.

Chapter 5 – Enhancing Influx, Diminishing Efflux

Now that you have acquired the skill of creating a budget, it is imperative that you adhere to it consistently. Whether you are confronted with a fiscal shortfall or desiring to enhance the surplus for greater savings, the ongoing pursuit of augmenting revenue inflow and mitigating outflow is an indispensable responsibility that warrants constant attention. Irrespective of your financial circumstances, it is imperative to consistently address them, even during periods of adequate budget surplus. By doing so, you shall safeguard against any potential deterioration of your surplus into a deficit.

This chapter aims to present various strategies for augmenting revenue and reducing expenses. While it is possible that not all of the examples outlined below may align precisely with your particular circumstances, they do possess the potential to stimulate creative thought processes aimed at enhancing your financial situation.

Ways to Cut Expenditure

In the following section, you will discover a valuable assortment of strategies for reducing unnecessary expenditures, arranged systematically according to categories. A few of the concepts that have been discussed are relatively uncomplicated and minor in scale; however, their potential to generate substantial profits in the long run is noteworthy, particularly when implemented alongside supplementary economic measures.

Please refrain from immediately dismissing any of these ideas. If the implementation of any of these options appears to entail a substantial alteration or sacrifice, we recommend considering the possibility of modifying it to a more amenable approach. One should demonstrate an attitude of acceptance towards all things; redirect your focus towards the benefits of reducing expenditures, rather than fixating on what you might miss out on. Occasionally, there are instances where one believes they cannot relinquish a specific endeavor, yet they come to the realization that they can thrive without it. Despite this, they may also acknowledge that abstaining from it actually enhances their overall well-being. As an illustration, opting for public transportation over utilizing your own vehicle affords you additional time for introspection, reading, or unwinding.

AVAIL CHEAP DEALS

Prior to delving into the particular facets of your domestic expenditures, it is imperative to provide you with a handful of recommendations to optimize the utilization of your financial resources, regardless of the nature of your disbursements. There are numerous exceptional online platforms that offer a comprehensive compilation of the most desirable promotions available in your local area. Whether you are seeking a bridal gown, an automobile, a plasma television, or a refrigerator, it is prudent to explore online for potential discounts prior to making any purchases. It is imperative to develop a practice of actively seeking discounts or promotions when making purchasing decisions, as this will undoubtedly lead to substantial long-term savings.

Here is another crucial recommendation concerning advertising: Make a consistent effort to purchase items during discounted periods, but exercise caution by refraining from making impulse purchases solely based on promotional offers. Instead of relying on the discount as a determining factor for your purchase, it is advisable to make your buying decisions solely based on necessity. When perusing the Sunday magazine with the intention of finding bargains and discounts, one is susceptible to the allure of buying superfluous items. Therefore, it is imperative not to overlook your budget while searching for advantageous offers. In the event that you are unable to abstain from making a purchase, it will be necessary to address this issue with your spending habits. The most effective approach to addressing this issue would involve solely seeking out bargains when one has a genuine need to make a purchase. Engaging with sales and advertisements outside of the context of practical necessity is likely to result in imprudent spending decisions.

What Strategies Can Be Employed to Reduce Grocery Expenses?

On average, individuals allocate approximately $250 per month towards grocery expenses. On average, a couple expends nearly twice the sum. When discussing the monthly expenses for a household consisting of four family members, the total amount can reach an astonishing $1200 per month. This represents a considerable sum. In the following discourse, you will encounter several recommendations to effectively reduce your grocery expenses by a significant margin of 20%.

Change Your Meals

Simple is good. Should you envision your evening repast as a nourishing banquet consisting of poultry and beef accompanied by a baguette and greens, supplemented by a confectionary indulgence in the form of chocolate cake, it behooves you to reevaluate your notion of a satisfactory culinary experience. The acquisition of costly groceries is not a prerequisite for achieving good taste and maintaining one's health and nutrition. Presented below is a comprehensive compilation of grocery items that can assist in reducing expenses while simultaneously preserving both nutritional value and flavor.

- Oatmeal
- Cream of Wheat
- Eggs
- Bread
- Cereal
- Bananas
- Apple
- Beans
- Lentils
- Rice
- Pasta
- Potatoes
- Sweet potatoes
- Carrots
- Canned Tomatoes
- Squash
- Zucchini
- Onions
- Broccoli
- Salsa
- Chicken
- Green Salad
- Spinach
- Ground Turkey
- Peanut Butter

Keep An Account As You Shop

While shopping at the grocery store and browsing through the aisles to gather your items, it is advisable to retrieve your phone from your pocket and access the calculator application. It is advised to continuously tally the prices of all selected products, as doing so will assist in adhering to the designated budget and prevent the acquisition of superfluous items. Furthermore, it will spare you the inconvenience of requesting deductions from your bill while the cashier finalizes your receipt.

Round-Up All the Prices

When placing an item in your shopping cart and calculating its price, it is advisable to round the cost to the nearest upper increment of 50 cents. For example, should an item be priced at $2.6, please add $3 to round it to $25.2. By doing so, you will ensure that you remain within the confines of the budget limit. Upon your final evaluation, you will be grateful to discover an additional amount of ten dollars at your disposal.

Exploit What You Have

There is perpetually a source available from which one can derive ingredients and prepare a meal. Examine the contents of your pantry and utilize your culinary creativity to devise diverse and inventive dishes using the available ingredients. There is no requirement for you to visit the supermarket given that you already possess several lamb ribs and canned beans within your refrigerator. Maximize the utilization of all available resources to their fullest extent. There exist a multitude of methods by which one can enhance the benefits derived from various food items.

Exercise Caution Prior to Engaging in Mass Purchases

Purchasing groceries in large quantities may initially appear to be a cost-effective choice. Prior to immersing oneself, it is prudent to consider which aquatic environments warrant a more preferable immersion. Do not hastily infer that purchasing in substantial volumes at discounted establishments necessarily results in lower costs. When adhering to a limited budget, please take a moment to engage in a thorough comparison of unit prices for the items you intend to purchase. It is highly alluring to accumulate supplies, however, there is truly no necessity to acquire more than what is required. Purchasing cereal in large quantities can prove advantageous when catering to a household with children; however, acquiring a 40-unit package of yoghurt would be wasteful for a couple or individuals.

Embrace the Convenience: Frozen Food as Your Unparalleled Ally

Greetings to freezer meals! The digital realm presents a plethora of freezer meal recipes that one can readily access and procure. Allocate a weekend to diligently assemble a selection of frozen meals, thereby ensuring a stress-free week ahead. Engaging in advanced preparations enables the implementation of the cost-effective purchasing approach and the preservation of precooked meals within freezer compartments. In addition to cost savings, it also facilitates time savings.

Ignore the Eye-level Products

Supermarkets strategically position higher-priced or aesthetically pleasing items within the aisles, aligning them with your field of vision as you traverse the store. Upon your next shopping excursion, take notice of how the conspicuously priced items are strategically positioned in plain view on the shelves. It is intentionally done, do not allow the grocers to undermine your determination. Avoid being swayed by deceptive marketing tactics such as these; instead, direct your attention to higher or lower shelves and make cost-effective purchasing choices. Remember this trick the next time you go shopping, better yet, write it down on the grocery list you've just made.

Don't Go Shopping Hungry

The sensation of hunger leads individuals to lose self-awareness, a phenomenon universally applicable. Many individuals are prone to committing a multitude of foolish errors when afflicted by hunger pangs. They have a tendency to make insincere statements, exhibit rapid anger, and impulsively gather any item that captures their attention while browsing the supermarket aisles. You may have been able to escape the consequences of other actions triggered by intense hunger, but your expenditure on groceries will not easily overlook or forgive you. Shop on a satiated stomach, ensuring that you only purchase necessary items.

Strategies for Reducing Transportation Expenses

Following housing costs, transportation expenses may rank as the second highest category of expenditure on your list. You may already be familiar with common approaches such as utilizing public transportation or cycling for commuting purposes; however, there exist lesser-known strategies that can effectively reduce your transportation expenses.

Weight Deduction!

This basic principle of physics has the potential to help you accumulate substantial savings in the long run. The additional mass in your vehicle is impeding its efficiency in covering a greater distance with a specific amount of fuel. One has the ability to promptly decrease the weight of one's car by up to 100 pounds, resulting in a potential enhancement of the vehicle's fuel efficiency by 3%.

A Well-maintained Car Saves Money.

Regularly maintaining your vehicle can result in a 4% increase in fuel efficiency. Maintaining the optimal air pressure in the tires can likewise enhance fuel efficiency by an equivalent percentage. Hence, by managing both these factors simultaneously, you can substantially improve your car's fuel efficiency by an impressive 8%.

Be Your Mechanic

Acquire knowledge in performing basic automotive maintenance tasks such as engine oil change and simple vehicle repairs. You have the opportunity to enroll in courses offered by a local community college or a skills training program within your vicinity. Alternatively, you may consider availing yourself of the option to view instructional videos on the platform of YouTube. You can acquire a diverse range of repair skills, from optimizing your car's performance to effectively replacing brake pads.

Drive Economically

By implementing alterations to your driving habits, you have the potential to achieve substantial financial savings. To begin with, exercise caution while operating the vehicle. Adhering to designated speed limits and practicing vigilant driving habits will help prevent the need for costly vehicle repairs and any potential penalties resulting from traffic violations. Furthermore, it is advised to maintain a maximum RPM of three while operating the vehicle. Refrain from accelerating in the initial two gears or during the commencement of the vehicle's motion. Consistently aim to increase velocity in a gradual manner. We advise minimizing brake utilization to the greatest extent possible; upon detecting an approaching red light, there is no practical benefit to maintaining pressure on the accelerator pedal only to abruptly engage the brakes upon reaching the signal. Allow your vehicle to decelerate naturally. This will help maintain the integrity of your brake system while promoting fuel efficiency.

Get Yourself a Bike

A bicycle is a highly favorable asset. Instead of initiating your vehicle when you are making a trip to town to obtain a loaf of bread, opt to employ your bicycle instead, which will result in monetary savings and the opportunity for physical activity.

Purchase your airline tickets promptly

It is essential to note that reserving your air travel at the last possible moment can result in substantial financial implications. In addition, it is advisable to take into account purchasing your flight tickets on a Monday or Tuesday, in the event that you make your reservation approximately one or two weeks prior to your desired travel date. Typically, the initial two days of the week tend to provide the most economical ticket prices in comparison to the remaining days of the week.

Carpool

By partaking in carpooling for your daily commute, you have the opportunity to reduce your travel expenses as well as minimize your carbon emissions. Various technological advancements are enabling the increased accessibility of carpooling, particularly for individuals employed by smaller organizations. There are a limited number of online platforms available that facilitate the sharing of commute arrangements among individuals employed within close proximity to each other.

In what manner can one reduce expenditures on apparel?

On average, the expenditure of clothing and accessories by the typical American amounts to around $1700 each year. If you want to manage your money, you certainly don't want to be spending this much on just clothes. Here is how you can save on clothing without sacrificing the quality of the garments you wear.

Buy Socks in Bulk

Despite the fact that purchasing socks in large quantities necessitates wearing the same color daily, opting for a classic black shade for men or standard skin tone socks for women in bulk will result in significant cost savings.

Make purchases during the conclusion of the season

Purchase now in anticipation of the upcoming year. By employing strategic planning and careful consideration, it would be advantageous to procure clothing for the impending winter during the spring clearance sale. Despite the immediate impracticality of immediate wear, you will be able to derive the benefits of your timely purchase in the upcoming year, accompanied by substantial cost savings.

Exchange Clothes with Pals

Upon the commencement of a season, you and your acquaintances have the opportunity to convene and engage in a collaborative exchange of garments that may no longer be of use to each of you. Arrange a designated day for trading among your acquaintances, whether they be friends or family, and proceed to dispose of any remaining garments. Earn a monetary income and acquire fresh garments.

Avoiding Unnecessary Expenses

Initially, it may appear challenging to abstain from unnecessary expenditures, yet it merely necessitates maintaining a consistent approach. Presented herein are several suggestions that can assist in mitigating superfluous expenditures.

1. Do not squander your financial resources on assurances

Take into consideration whether the individual warranties being offered are truly of significant value when considering the associated costs. Certainly, it is worth noting that certain guarantees may not provide substantial value in proportion to their associated costs. Therefore, it is advisable to exercise caution, particularly when dealing with electronics.

Upon purchasing an electronic device, such as a television, headphones, or computer, we are promptly presented with the option to acquire an extended warranty. The issue arises from the fact that the cost associated with acquiring this guarantee can at times amount to one third of the overall expense of the item, a figure that is notably excessive.

Kindly inquire prior to making a purchase regarding an extended warranty, as many devices are typically already provided with a manufacturer's warranty.

2. Purchasing lottery tickets, an extraneous expenditure to be avoided

Do you possess the detrimental tendency of expending funds on one or more lottery tickets on a weekly basis?

Given the exceedingly slim odds of achieving a substantial financial gain through participating in the lottery, this expenditure is utterly devoid of practical value. It is advisable to refrain from participating in the lottery if one intends to save funds on a weekly basis.

The likelihood of winning in the lottery is exceedingly low, rendering it unjustifiable to invest your money in such a manner.

3. It is advised against purchasing the most recent model of the phone.

Do you belong to the category of individuals who exhibit a penchant for consistently procuring the latest iterations of electronic devices or mobile phones upon their initial release?

Given the annual release of new models, such as in the realm of game consoles and phones, one might feel inclined to make the switch to the latest iteration.

It would be prudent to refrain from incurring this superfluous expenditure, given the marginal modifications typically made to the majority of devices. Typically, it represents an improvement to the camera in the majority of instances. Exercise self-control and refrain from purchasing a new phone, thus preserving financial resources for an additional year.

4. Slot machines should be avoided!

Slot machines found in certain establishments and even accessible through online platforms possess the potential to result in significant financial losses. In fact, all associated elements of casinos invariably lead to substantial monetary depletion. It is imperative to acknowledge that the establishment unfailingly emerges victorious, and it would be prudent for one to bear this wisdom in mind. They have been artfully designed to create an illusion of opportunity, despite the lack thereof.

5. The coffee procured from the restaurant of your daily preference!

Rather than expending a daily sum ranging from 3 to 5 dollars on a basic cup of coffee, avail yourself of the opportunity to prepare your coffee at home and acquire a thermos to conveniently carry it with you.

A small suggestion that effortlessly reduces expenses by an estimated amount of 10 to 20 dollars per week, and potentially even more for certain individuals.

6. The newspaper - an additional superfluous expenditure

Papers incur significant costs! By quantifying the expenditure over an entire year, for instance, it becomes evident that a substantial sum of money is involved.

Considering the fact that you have access to internet facilities both at your place of residence and your workplace, it seems unnecessary to allocate additional funds towards purchasing a newspaper. Peruse the latest news articles on your mobile device or tablet—a straightforward task indeed!

7. Cigarettes - an expenditure to steer clear of!

Smoking cigarettes is detrimental to your health. Not only do they inflict harm upon your respiratory system, but they also result in a significant depletion of financial resources. The government has imposed a series of taxes on cigarettes, thus avoiding the necessity of spending such a substantial amount on them. It is merely an unfavorable tendency, and it would be advisable to relinquish it.

Furthermore, aside from their detrimental health effects, cigarettes impose a significant financial burden. If you happen to be a smoker, it is unquestionably a superfluous expenditure that ought to be promptly dispensed with.

8. The landline phone

Are you currently subscribed to a mobile phone service? A considerable number of individuals possess a cellular device, thus questioning the necessity of continuing to incur monthly expenses for a landline telephone.

The cost of a fixed line package can exceed $20, contingent upon the selected options. Therefore, envision the considerable amount of savings that can be realized by terminating this monthly package.

9. Stop spending on restaurants!

For individuals who are employed outside of their residences, the allure of dining at a restaurant alongside their co-workers can be quite compelling, wouldn't you agree? Consuming meals at the restaurant on a daily basis, or even indulging in this practice once a week, can significantly strain one's financial resources. It is advisable to prepare your lunch in the morning upon awakening, as this practice can result in substantial financial savings on a weekly basis.

10. Cut into parking lots

Parking facilities can be financially burdensome; therefore, it is advisable to carefully examine alternative modes of transportation, such as cycling or utilizing public transit options like the Metro, buses, parking meters, and trains, as these options offer a plethora of alternatives. It is imperative to engage in thorough calculations in order to ascertain that the cost does not amount to an equivalent or higher figure.

www.ingramcontent.com/pod-product-compliance
Lightning Source LLC
Chambersburg PA
CBHW050244120526
44590CB00016B/2209